THE FUTURE OF FOOD

New Ideas About Eating

Toney Allman

ReferencePoint Press

San Diego, CA

© 2021 ReferencePoint Press, Inc.
Printed in the United States

For more information, contact:
ReferencePoint Press, Inc.
PO Box 27779
San Diego, CA 92198
www.ReferencePointPress.com

LIBRARY OF CONGRESS CATALOGING-IN-PUBLICATION DATA

Names: Allman, Toney, author.
Title: The future of food : new ideas about eating / by Toney Allman.
Description: San Diego : ReferencePoint Press, 2021. | Includes
    bibliographical references and index.
Identifiers: LCCN 2020001485 (print) | LCCN 2020001486 (ebook) | ISBN
    9781682829271 (library binding) | ISBN 9781682829288 (ebook)
Subjects: LCSH: Food supply--Juvenile literature. | Food industry and
    trade--Forecasting--Juvenile literature. | Nutrition--Juvenile
    literature.
Classification: LCC HD9000.5 .A454 2021 (print) | LCC HD9000.5 (ebook) |
    DDC 338.1/9--dc23
LC record available at https://lccn.loc.gov/2020001485
LC ebook record available at https://lccn.loc.gov/2020001486

CONTENTS

Future Food Issues

The world's population is growing, and along with it, the need for adequate, nutritious food supplies. According to the Institute on the Environment at the University of Minnesota, there is enough food today to provide the calorie needs of the earth's 7 billion people, but by 2050, with more than 9 billion people predicted, the problem will be ensuring a nutritious diet for all while minimizing damage to the planet and its ecosystems.

Writing for the World Economic Forum, Juergen Voegele and Jane Nelson argue, "Finding solutions to provide nutritious food to nearly 10 billion people by 2050 without destroying our planet is one of the greatest leadership opportunities of our generation."[1] The necessity of finding these solutions is a major driver in today's efforts to develop worldwide changes in food production and farming practices, as well as in the types of food people consume. In 1948 the United Nations adopted the Universal Declaration of Human Rights, which included the right to adequate food for everyone, but that goal has not yet been realized and may be even more difficult to achieve in the future.

The Issue of Enough Food for All

Food security means having access to enough nutritious food both to meet people's preferences in types of food and to enable them to sustain a healthy, active life. Today, despite adequate food production, 820 million people are undernourished because of unequal food distribution. They are food insecure. Many of these people are victims of war, displacement, or political neglect and corruption. The Food and Agriculture Organization of the United Nations (FAO) reports that others are food insecure due to extreme weather events, climate change, land that is so overused that it can't sustain animals or crops, and lack of access to enough water. To change this situation and ensure that everyone receives an adequate diet by 2050, new methods of growing and distributing foods will be needed because food production will have to double.

At the same time that millions of people are food insecure, millions of others in the developing world are escaping poverty. Many are becoming more prosperous, and as they do, they demand better nutrition and a greater variety of healthy foods. A Food Matters report from the Institute on the Environment explains, "Richer people tend to want richer foods, including meat and dairy products."[2] These people want more food and in greater variety, so as more of them escape poverty, they create an increased demand for more food. This is why food production will have to double by 2050, even though the population grows by only one-third.

> "Finding solutions to provide nutritious food to nearly 10 billion people . . . is one of the greatest leadership opportunities of our generation."[1]
>
> —Juergen Voegele and Jane Nelson of the World Economic Forum

The Issue of Planetary Protection

People in the developing world, however, are not the only ones who need better nutrition. In the developed world, people have plenty to eat, but they often eat too much overall or not enough of the right kinds of foods. These people, too, seek and require healthy, convenient food options. More and more of them also demand that the environment be protected from the strain food production places on the land and the climate. As the Scottish Food Coalition explains:

> Many factors including farming method, where food is grown, what pesticides and fertilisers are used, what is fed to our livestock, and so on, affect the environmental impact of the food we buy and eat. . . . And what about climate change? Around one-third of global greenhouse gas emissions come from agriculture, so our food system needs to take a big role in tackling climate change.[3]

Protecting the environment while providing all the world's people with ample, healthy food may seem like an impossible challenge. "Luckily," say Voegele and Nelson, "we're beginning

Many people who suffer from food insecurity are victims of war, displacement, or political neglect and corruption.

to see plausible, scientifically rigorous solutions emerge to make the food system more inclusive, sustainable, efficient and nutritious."[4] Standards of living do not necessarily have to be reduced to protect the planet from detrimental human activity. Millions of people may, in fact, be able to see their standard of living raised and to become food secure. Experts in human health, food production, and environmental resources do predict that changing our diets and our tastes in foods, accepting different kinds of foods, and reducing food loss and waste in agriculture will be necessary. However, such changes need not be a hardship. Already, science, technology, and medicine are pointing the way to this future.

"Around one-third of global greenhouse gas emissions come from agriculture, so our food system needs to take a big role in tackling climate change."[3]

—Scottish Food Coalition

CHAPTER ONE

How the World Gets Its Food

The world's food comes primarily from farming, fishing, and the raising of livestock. Experts warn that traditional practices in each of these areas may fall short of future food needs while also depleting the land and water that yield all of this food.

Crop Farming

Crop farming, for example, is dominated by large-scale agriculture. Whether run by corporations or families, large-scale farming generally entails more than 1,000 acres (405 ha) of cropland and the use of intensive agricultural practices. It is a highly productive farming method. Large-scale family farms in the United States account for 42 percent of agricultural production each year, even though they represent only 10 percent of family farms. Large farms owned by corporations account for another 11 percent of production. Large-scale farms outperform small-scale farms worldwide in efficiency, profitability, and the abundance of crop yields. They are able to produce more food per acre than any small farm can accomplish because they can take advantage of industrial methods, techniques, and technologies to achieve the best results.

Intensive farmers plant multiple crops each year on the same acreage, which necessitates extensive use of fertilizers, pesticides, herbicides (weed killers), and highly efficient

8

agricultural machinery to plant, maintain, irrigate, and reap the crops. Intensive, large-scale farming also typically means monoculture or monocropping. This means planting the same crop on the same land year after year. Intensive farming on a large scale has been a huge success story in one sense. It is feeding much of the world abundantly. Just fifteen plant crops today provide 90 percent of the world's food energy needs, and just three crops—wheat, corn, and rice—account for 66 percent of this, providing the staple foods for 4 billion people.

This success story, however, has come with a cost. The FAO explains, "Agricultural production is limited by the increasing

Large-scale farms produce more food per acre than small farms, thanks, in part, to modern machinery.

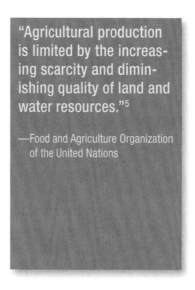

scarcity and diminishing quality of land and water resources. . . . Climate change is increasingly affecting yields and rural livelihoods, while agriculture continues to emit greenhouse gases."[5] Most of the world's land suitable for farming is already in use and at capacity. Intensive monocropping degrades and depletes the soil of nutrients. Pesticides and fertilizers pollute the land and water and contribute to greenhouse gas emissions, as does farm machinery. The world's few staple crops are extremely vulnerable to climate changes that may lead to crop failure as temperatures rise or water supplies fail. All of these factors make today's large-scale farming unsustainable and incapable of feeding future generations.

A Better Way

The nonprofit Union of Concerned Scientists says, "A growing number of innovative farmers and scientists are . . . moving toward a farming system that is more sustainable—environmentally, economically, and socially. This system has room for farms of all sizes." All agricultural practices can be improved, whether the farm operates on just a few acres or is a huge corporate enterprise. Farmland can be protected and even enhanced in several ways. The Union of Concerned Scientists explains further, "Environmental sustainability in agriculture means good stewardship of the natural systems and resources that farms rely on. Among other things, this involves:

- Building and maintaining healthy soil
- Managing water wisely
- Minimizing air, water, and climate pollution
- Promoting biodiversity."[6]

Many organic farmers in the United States practice sustainable farming. In addition to shunning the use of pesticides and herbicides, they concentrate on improving the soil by using a no-till system. Tilling degrades the soil by disturbing the microorganisms that feed plants, destroying deep roots that hold soil in place, and causing erosion. Levi Lyle is an Iowa organic no-till farmer. Instead of plowing and tilling his fields to prepare them for planting, he plants cover crops of cereal rye. Then he uses a piece of machinery called a roller crimper to squash the cover crop flat. Lyle explains, "It lays down and serves as a mat thick enough to inhibit weed growth, providing an excellent herbicide

A Sustainable Hog Farm

Jan and Steve Petersen run a family farm in Decatur, Michigan, where they are committed to protecting the land for future generations and raising animals humanely. Their hay and corn crops are grown following sustainable agriculture practices, and their hogs are raised naturally and unconfined. The Petersens say, "Pigs spend their entire lives in pastures, with metal Quonset huts for shelter. We have always rotated pastures and crops, using mostly organic practices. We rotate pastures and crops and never allow livestock near the creek that runs through our farm." The farmers keep their water resources unpolluted by animal waste, use pig manure to fertilize their crops, and maintain natural wild, wooded areas on the farm to benefit wildlife. The Petersens are pleased that people in general are becoming more and more interested in how their food animals are raised, even if it means their meat costs a little more. The Petersens love all the land of their farm and are determined to protect it and avoid overusing or depleting the soil of nutrients. They say, "We always hope the wildlife appreciates our commitment to avoid farming the whole place into the ground."

Quoted in Katherine Walla, "Farming Better Isn't Enough: We Need to Protect Land," Foodtank, 2018. https://foodtank.com.

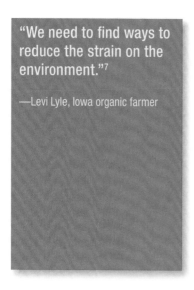

alternative. Cereal rye is also great for soil health and nitrogen uptake." Lyle plants his cash crops of soybeans or corn directly into the matted cover. He says that this system both eliminates soil erosion and is profitable. He argues for all farmers, "We need to find ways to reduce the strain on the environment."[7] He is building healthy soil and reducing the chemicals that pollute the earth.

In Australia the double issues of regular, prolonged droughts and intensive farming methods have left farmers struggling with repeated complete crop failures. To combat this, the nonprofit Mulloon Institute promotes a system called natural sequence farming, with the goal of returning water to farmlands and making them sustainable. In 2013 the institute started the Mulloon Community Landscape Rehydration Project, which involves twenty-three farmers along more than 31 miles (50 km) of Mulloon Creek, a devastated, badly eroded, mostly dry creek bed. Together the project leaders and farmers are building "leaky weirs" across the creek, using rocks, fallen tree limbs, and other natural debris to slow but not stop the trickle of water running down the creek. This makes some of the water seep into the landscape on either side of the creek, where the farmers plant reeds, blackberries, and other weed plants. They plant willows, too, which most farmers consider nuisance trees. The roots of these native Australian plants sink deep into the soil, providing stability against erosion.

As the surrounding land and creek return to their natural state, the earth begins to act like a natural sponge that soaks up water. As time passes and the "sponge" fills up, the water slowly seeps back toward the creek, where some remains, even during dry periods. Side branches form with flowing water that spreads across the agricultural acreage. Peter Andrews, one of the founders of the Mulloon Institute, explains, "All we've done is reproduced what was a natural process in Australia's landscapes. We've been able to get water into the floodplains which sustains the landscape in a drought."[8]

In 2019 the project was awarded a $3.8 million government grant to continue its work and establish a scientific basis for expanding natural sequence farming in Australia. Gary Nairn, chair of the Mulloon Institute, says, "We want to say to farmers and governments that we have a solution—we have a way to rehydrate and regenerate the Australian landscape and make our landscapes more resilient to extreme climatic conditions."[9]

Livestock Farming

Some of the farmers living along Mulloon Creek raise livestock as well as crops, and they are discovering that their grazing lands are benefiting from natural sequence farming, too. Sustainable practices are just as important for raising livestock as they are for raising crops. Conventional large-scale intensive livestock rearing,

Intensive livestock farming concentrates on raising large numbers of animals, such as these pigs, in confined spaces.

also sometimes called factory farming, carries much of the same environmental cost as crop farming does. It concentrates on raising large numbers of animals, such as cows, chickens, and pigs, in confined spaces to maximize production and minimize cost. Generally, only one type of animal is raised on a farm, either for meat, milk, or eggs. Cheap feed is brought in to feed the animals rather than allowing them to graze or roam free. Animal manure and waste is usually stored in large lagoons instead of being recycled as fertilizer. Antibiotics are liberally fed to the animals so that

Poisonous Fish Farms?

Tilapia are a white-fleshed, mild-tasting fish that are easy to raise on fish farms. Although some are raised in farms in North America, most are imported from Asia, especially China. In the United States some 82 percent of tilapia comes from China. Investigative reporting over the past several years has revealed that many of these fish are raised in filthy conditions, leading many consumers to fear buying and eating them. Many reports reveal that the fish are fed the feces of chickens and other animals and that the ponds where the fish are grown are dirty and polluted. In addition, because of the dirty conditions, the fish are fed heavy doses of antibiotics to prevent disease.

The US Food and Drug Administration (FDA) denies that there is any evidence that imported tilapia are fed feces, but even in clean fish ponds, the fish are fed soy and corn instead of their natural, healthy diet of algae. Professor Joseph Schwarcz of McGill University in Canada states that it is unclear how commonly Asian fish farms are contaminated with feces, and the feces-feeding practice cannot be proved. Nevertheless, he says, while farm-raised tilapia are not as healthy as wild-caught tilapia, they can still be part of a healthy diet. He recommends choosing fish from North America when possible. Other experts recommend tilapia farmed in Ecuador, Peru, Mexico, Indonesia, and Taiwan.

their crowded conditions do not lead to the spread of disease. Intensive animal farming is a cheap, efficient method of providing meat, milk, and eggs. About 94 percent of meat animals raised in the United States are raised on factory farms.

Such concentrated animal feeding operations, however, will not be sustainable. Environmentally, these farms are a large source of pollution, both of the soil and of waterways and even oceans. Dead zones in oceans, for example, are areas with such low levels of oxygen that no ocean life can survive in them. They are often caused by accidental spills from the lagoons of animal waste or uncontrolled runoff of polluted water from farms. The nutrients in these wastes feed algae, causing huge algal blooms that use up the oxygen. The widespread use of antibiotics to prevent, rather than treat, disease is also unsustainable. The United Kingdom's environmental advocacy group Farm Health Online explains, "This practice contributes to the emergence and spread of resistant bacteria in both animal and human populations. Resistant microorganisms carried by food-producing animals can spread to humans through consumption of contaminated food, from direct contact with animals, or via the environment (e.g., contaminated water)."[10] A world in which infectious diseases spread unchecked because antibiotics do not work anymore is hardly a healthy world.

In addition, the land on which animal feed is grown for confined animals is depleted of nutrients that are never returned by grazing animals that spread manure back into the soil. Factory farms are closed, unnatural systems—in which even the livestock is unhealthy—and provide less-than-optimal nutrition for the people who eat the meat and dairy products the farms produce.

Sustainable Beef Production

Cattle, say some researchers, have a particularly large and negative impact on the planet. Cattle ranching is blamed not only for land and water degradation but also for adding to greenhouse gas emissions. Some studies show that the methane released as gas from cattle's digestive processes is responsible for as much as 18 percent of the greenhouse gas emissions that contribute to climate change. Yet, that devastating effect may not be because there are too many cattle in the world. It may be caused by how cattle are raised. One scientist, Alexander N. Hristov, calculated the amount of methane released by wild populations of bison, elk, and deer in history before they were replaced by domestic animals. Hristov determined that the methane emissions from wild herds were the same as is emitted today. Just as many wild herds existed as there are cattle today. They produced just as much methane. So the question is why did ancient herds not cause climate change when cattle of today are causing a problem, and why are the results of methane emission so different?

A research team at Michigan State University offers an answer. The university runs a cattle farm that uses adaptive multi-paddock (AMP) grazing methods instead of the traditional intensive farming feedlots to fatten cattle for market. AMP grazing involves allowing cattle to graze in a large pasture but confining them to specific sections of the pasture with movable fencing. Once the cattle have intensively grazed one section, they are moved to another section so the grasses in the grazed section can recover. The researchers found that this method is healthier for cattle, allowing them to digest their food better and release less methane. At the same time, the animals naturally fertilize the pasture soil with their manure, which adds carbon. Carbon added to and trapped in the soil is carbon not released into the air, and that is a good thing for the planet.

Allen Williams and Russ Conser, agricultural experts, conclude, "Now that we see the bigger picture, we intuitively know that the wild ruminants [cud-chewing animals such as buffalo, elk, and deer] of the past were pumping more carbon into the soil than they were emitting into the air. A ruminant-filled planet thrived before us, and it can again today. . . . We now have measured data demonstrating that good grazing can be a net win for both your farm and the overall environment."[11] Farmers using AMP methods sell their meat as grass-fed beef or pasture-raised beef, make a profit, and are able to state that they practice regenerative farming that is environmentally friendly.

Farmers raising other food animals, such as chickens and hogs, are developing sustainable methods that are environmentally friendly as well. Terry Baker, for instance, is a large-scale chicken farmer in Delaware. He says, "I think it is our responsibility as farmers to be good stewards of the environment."[12] Baker practices water conservation with a large pond surrounded by grasses and weeds to catch rainwater and absorb nutrients from feed or waste manure that might leach into the pond. He recycles 100 percent of the chickens' litter and manure, selling it to other farmers for natural fertilizer. He plants weeds and bushes between each chicken house to capture dust and other particles and the ammonia from chicken manure that could pollute the air. Many chicken farms employ such practices today. The National Chicken Council reports, "Chicken production has a smaller environmental footprint than almost any other animal agriculture industry, and we are continuing to develop and advance our sustainable and environmentally-friendly practices so that we leave the earth in better shape than we found it."[13]

> "Chicken production has a smaller environmental footprint than almost any other animal agriculture industry."[13]
>
> —National Chicken Council

Fishing for Food

The fishing industry is another major source of the world's food supply. It provides the quality protein on which some 3 billion people depend. Approximately half of the fish supply is wild caught, while the other half is raised in fish farms. In 2017 more than 101 billion tons (92 billion metric tons) of fish were wild caught and sold for human consumption worldwide. The fish stocks in the oceans in particular, however, are in danger, and marine experts warn that this overfishing is unsustainable. The FAO states that one-third of ocean species are in decline, and almost 90 percent of all species are at the edge of sustainability.

Aquaculture, or fish farming, could become a sustainable way to feed the world and reduce the pressure on the oceans in the future, but today consumption of fish has risen throughout the world so that both wild fishing and fish farming are needed to meet demand. Stefano Longo, a sociology professor at North Carolina State University, studied the situation and says, "We found that aquaculture has expanded production, but does not appear to be advancing fishery conservation. . . . In other words, aquaculture is not taking the place of traditional fishing efforts, or even necessarily reducing them."[14]

Nevertheless, insists the global aquaculture company BioMar, fish farming is the most efficient form of meat production to feed the world and is on track to becoming the most sustainable. The two major methods of fish farming are open net systems and

Fishing provides high-quality protein for billions of people, but experts warn that fish stocks in the world's oceans are in serious danger.

closed systems. Open net systems are pens built to hold fish in lakes or along coastlines. The fish are raised in these pens until large enough to harvest. The problem with this system is that it may harm the environment. Chemicals or antibiotics used in raising the fish can escape into the surrounding water. Any diseases that may come from breeding fish in close quarters can spread to surrounding wild populations. The fish can escape as well. In 2017, 160,000 Atlantic salmon, for example, escaped through a broken pen into the Pacific Ocean. This nonnative species invasion of the Pacific poses a threat to the native salmon. The accident raises questions about the sustainability of open net aquaculture.

The World's Best Hope?

Closed systems, on the other hand, involve raising fish on land in large tanks or ponds, with recirculation systems for the water to keep it clean and avoid polluting the environment. The Nelson family, for instance, are fish farmers in Iowa, raising a species of grouper called barramundi that is native to Australia. The fish adapt well to the large tanks in which they are raised and demand much less food and care than cattle or hogs. As an example, to produce 1 pound (454 g) of beef requires about 10 pounds (4.5 kg) of feed and 1,000 gallons (3,785 L) of water. To produce 1 pound of barramundi requires only 1 pound of grain and 7 gallons (26.5 L) of water. Mark Nelson comments, "You look at that stuff and it's like, okay, this is a good way to go if we're going to continue to feed the world."[15] Such fish farming is not yet widespread, either in Iowa or throughout the world, but many believe it may be the only way to ensure that the oceans survive. Aquaculture is just one farming practice that could provide abundant food while protecting ecosystems. Sustainable agriculture, whether in fish farming, crop farming, or livestock production, could both feed the world and save the planet.

CHAPTER TWO

Meat Alternatives

In 2019 the fast-food company Burger King introduced its Impossible Whopper, a meatless sandwich made with a vegetarian burger patty instead of beef. The company hopes to draw people into its restaurants who usually avoid fast-food offerings either because they eschew meat or they desire healthier food options. This is not the first time that a fast-food chain has tried to introduce a meatless burger. McDonald's, for example, tried serving veggie burgers in the past but gave up on the idea because they did not sell. In 2011 its chief executive officer (CEO), Don Thompson, complained, "We ended up serving four a day."[16] Burger King's burger, however, is a new kind of vegetarian burger. So far, it is highly successful. All restaurant sales increased by 5 percent after it was introduced. Many customers insist that the Impossible Whopper tastes just like the real thing.

Toward Reducing Meat Consumption

Burger King's goal with the Impossible Whopper is to increase its profit by increasing its customer base, but this is possible only because so many Americans are rethinking their eating habits. According to a 2018 Gallup poll, about 5 percent of Americans identify themselves as vegetarian, while about 3 percent say they are vegan. These numbers have remained virtually unchanged over the past twenty years. Worldwide, the average is about the same—approximately 5 percent of people are vegetarian by choice. However, a 2018 study of more than one thousand adults found that two-thirds reported reducing their meat consumption over a period of three years. Some of these people opt for regular meatless meals; others report eating less red meat; still others reduced their consumption of processed meats. In most cases the reason for reducing meat is health concerns, but other reasons include concerns about the environment or the treatment of animals. People are becoming more concerned that livestock rearing may be a source of pollution or a contributor to climate change. They are interested in the possible health benefits of eating less meat. And they worry that farm animals are treated inhumanely.

Fueling the willingness to reduce meat consumption are the many scientific efforts to develop acceptable, healthy, and satisfying alternatives to today's meat choices. The introduction of the Impossible Whopper, for instance, was made possible by Burger King's partnership with the company Impossible Foods, which has been developing the plant-based burger since the company was founded in 2011.

Impossible Goals

Impossible Foods was started by California biochemistry professor Patrick Brown. Recognizing that the company's success was impossible without developing a product that even meat eaters

Vegetarian burgers are becoming increasingly popular as American consumers are increasingly concerned about the health effects of eating meat and the environmental costs of producing meat.

would love, he and his team of scientists analyzed meat at the molecular level to understand exactly where its taste comes from. They wanted to develop a burger patty that looks, smells, feels, and tastes just like ground beef. The scientists determined that the chemical compound in meat that gives it its flavor is heme. Heme is a component of the protein hemoglobin in the blood. Heme is the part of the hemoglobin molecule that gives blood its color, and it is rich in the iron that gives meat much of its taste. Meat is rich in heme, but as it turns out, a form of heme exists in some plants, too, such as the roots of soybeans. Using yeast to ferment and grow this heme in large quantities and combining the result with soy protein, oils, and other ingredients, Impossible Foods developed a product that seems to "bleed" like real meat and taste like it, too.

Brown's goal is to put an end to the meat and dairy industry by 2035. He explains:

> I decided to found the company because I recognized that the use of animals as a food production technology is by far the most destructive technology on Earth. . . . The use of animals as a food production technology is responsible for more greenhouse gas emissions than the entire transportation system. . . . This technology uses more water and pollutes more water than any other technology by far. It also now occupies almost half of Earth's entire land area, either for growing crops to feed animals or for grazing land. Livestock has essentially pushed all the diverse wildlife that used to exist on the planet to the edge of extinction. Cows alone far outweigh every other terrestrial mammal left on earth.[17]

Beyond Meat Aspirations

Brown believes that meat substitutes are the only way to save the planet while feeding the world's growing population. The ground beef substitute that goes into the Impossible Whopper was introduced into grocery stores in September 2019, and at least some people are accepting it and making the product successful. And Impossible Foods is not the only company working on reducing

Algae Instead

Algae—or microalgae, as scientists refer to them—are single-celled organisms in the same family as seaweed. Thousands of different varieties of algae exist, and many of them are edible. They can grow almost anywhere, including on a pond or in the ocean. Algae have long been a food source in certain parts of Asia and Central America, but farmed commercially in tanks, ponds, or labs, algae have the potential to feed the world. Algae are extremely high in protein, vitamins, and the omega-3 fatty acids often missing in the diets of vegetarians and vegans. They grow fast, require minimal space, and need just a few nutrients plus sunlight to multiply.

In New Mexico a company called iWi is farming microalgae that are already commercially available as a source of omega-3 for supplements and as an additive to protein powders. Someday, however, the company believes algae will revolutionize food. Founder and CEO Miguel Calatayud explains, "Algae is going to be part of a regular food chain for us. It's going to be a great thing for all of us and for our planet." In the future, without algae, he says, "there will not be enough animal protein or other vegetable protein. There won't be enough arable land, and what's even more important, there won't be enough fresh water." If people have algae to eat, however, there will be enough healthy food for all.

Quoted in Rachel Crane, "Experts Say Algae Is the Food of the Future. Here's Why," CNN Business, June 1, 2018. https://money.cnn.com.

meat consumption and producing plant-based products that taste like meat. Beyond Meat was founded in 2009 by its CEO, Ethan Brown (no relation to Patrick Brown), to fight climate change by developing alternative, plant-based products. The company produces and sells sausage, chicken-free strips, and beefless burgers and ground crumbles. Although Ethan Brown wants to see people give up meat eventually, he says, "We are not telling people not to eat meat—I think that would be a massive mistake—we're simply suggesting that they have a new type of meat, just plant based. . . . Once we break the code and get to the point where it's indistinguishable from animal protein, I think you will see that shift."[18]

Brown's reference to "code" means he still does not believe he has figured out all the ways to make plant-based foods taste exactly like meat, even though his products are successful. Beyond Meat's foods are sold in restaurants such as Carl's Jr. and in some grocery stores, but he is not satisfied with them. He says that the

Companies such as Beyond Meat continue to research ways to make their products look and taste just like real meat.

smell is not quite right, the distribution of fats needs to be improved, and the color is too red. The research team at Beyond Meat is working on further innovations. The ingredients of Beyond Meat products are different from the Impossible Foods burger. They include plant foods such as mung beans, rice, pea proteins, and beet juice to make the meatless foods seem to bleed. Researchers are satisfied with the basic ingredients but continue to tweak which and how much of each is used. Brown explains:

"We are not telling people not to eat meat . . . we're simply suggesting that they have a new type of meat, just plant based."[18]

—Ethan Brown, founder of Beyond Meat

We are on this mission to build a perfect piece of meat. . . . We have to prove that we can do this because the only thing that I know with absolute certainty about the consumer is that the consumer loves meat. You know most of us do. Around 94 percent of the population here in United States. . . . You know our hope and our dream is that we'll continue as a species to go on loving and consuming meat. Maybe that's plant based meat.[19]

How About Insects?

Plant-based meat, however, may not be the only path toward protecting the planet and reducing the conventional meat consumption of today. Maybe, suggest some researchers, insect farming is the food innovation of the future. Some researchers and companies are exploring and developing insects as meat substitutes. Wild-caught insects already make up part of the diets of some 2 billion people around the world. Alan-Javier Hernandez-Alvarez of the University of Leeds in the United Kingdom says, "Edible insects could be the solution to the problem of how to meet the growing global demand for food in a sustainable way. [But] the

Edible insects, such as these fried crickets, are high in protein and have good levels of micronutrients such as iron and zinc.

'ick factor' remains one of the biggest barriers to edible insects becoming the norm."[20]

Setting squeamishness aside, the benefits of insect farming become obvious. Edible insects are highly nutritious. They are extremely high in protein, have good levels of micronutrients such as iron and zinc, and provide healthy polyunsaturated fats. Yet they are extremely low in calories. They could be raised in large numbers, both indoors and out, as they require very little space, placing minimal stress on the world's land and water resources. Producing 1 pound (454 g) of protein from insects requires 2 pounds (907 g) of feed, 1 gallon (3.8 L) of water, and 2 cubic feet (56,634 cu. cm) of land. In contrast, producing 1 pound of beef uses 10 pounds (4.5 kg) of feed, 1,000 gallons (3,785 L) of water, and 200 square feet (18.6 sq. m) of grazing land.

A switch to consumption of edible insects also might hugely reduce greenhouse gas emissions and thereby help reduce climate change. Crickets and mealworms produce 1 percent of the amount of greenhouse gases produced by cattle. Some edible insects can even be grown in and fed on waste products, thus reducing environmental pollution by recycling products such as the grain left over from making beer or expired fruits and vegetables from grocery stores. Miha Pipan, scientific officer of the company Entomics, is an enthusiastic advocate for the benefits of insect farming with wastes, both to feed humanity and to save the planet. He explains, "Insects have an immense potential in help[ing] humanity deal with facing the threat of climate change and food production resilience. From the inherently low usage of land, to the ability of insects eating decomposing wastes (which is a major cause of methane emissions worldwide), to the marginal lower water usage per kilo of protein produced. I could go on for a while on this topic."[21]

> "Edible insects could be the solution to the problem of how to meet the growing global demand for food in a sustainable way."[20]
>
> —Alan-Javier Hernandez-Alvarez of the University of Leeds

Bug Companies

Although no one is practicing large-scale insect farming yet, some of the insects already being farmed on a small scale around the world include crickets, mealworms, black soldier flies, grasshoppers, silkworms, and cicadas. Bugfoundation is a European company that sells a burger in several countries that is made of buffalo worms cultivated in the Netherlands. One of the company founders, Max Kramer, explains, "The insects are crushed to obtain paste and other vegetarian ingredients are added to the mix, such as onions and tomato paste."[22] The popular frozen insect burger has been sold in supermarkets in Germany since 2018, and curious and interested consumers there seem willing to buy and eat it. Bugfoundation has even had a difficult time supplying stores because its production cannot keep up with the demand. That situation seems to indicate that people can overcome any feelings that insects are too gross to eat. The company says that its insect burgers are delicious and have a rich, nutty flavor.

Another way to overcome resistance to eating insects might be to turn them into a flour or powder. This is what the company Chirps has done. It makes cookie mix and protein chips out of milled cricket powder. Journalist Kendrick Foster sat down with his family at the dinner table one day with a bag of cricket chips for everyone to try. His mother agreed to try one. His father ate a few and thought they were not too bad. His brother refused to try them at all because the idea was disgusting to him. Foster reports, "Meanwhile, I chomp away at the remaining chips, having looked forward to this admittedly unusual snack for a while."[23] Perhaps cricket chips are not for everyone, but this kind of snack may become more acceptable to more people in the future. Aly Moore, a public health educator and enthusiastic advocate of insect eating, suggests, "We're trying to rebrand [the ick factor] to the wow factor, in a similar way to a roller coaster. You're terrified of it, and it's scary, but after you do it, it's super fun and really cool."[24]

Real Meat from the Lab

If people are unwilling to give up meat in favor of plants or insects, perhaps the sustainable alternative is lab-grown meat, made from the cells of living animals. Also known as synthetic meat or cultured meat, lab-grown meat is not yet ready for commercial sale, but a few companies are working diligently to produce an affordable and tasty product. The meat is produced by harvesting a small sample of muscle tissue from a living animal. The procedure is painless and harmless to the animal. In the laboratory, stem cells are extracted from the tissue sample. Stem cells are the special cells in all bodies from which other

cells, such as skin and muscle cells, grow. When skin cells are damaged—for instance, from a cut—the body's stem cells rush to the site of the injury, multiply, and turn into skin cells to heal the wound. Stem cells from a cow similarly can specialize into muscle cells and theoretically can be kept multiplying by the billions to form muscle tissue. Today these stem cells are placed in a growth medium of cow's blood, where they multiply until they form small strips of muscle tissue—meat.

The first hamburger made of lab-grown meat was developed in 2013. It cost $325,000 to produce, and according to tasters it was not very good. It tasted odd and was dry because of a lack of fat cells, but it was a start. If scientists can figure out a way to

Lab-Grown Fish

In a laboratory in San Diego, California, a company called BlueNalu has created lab-grown fish, specifically yellowtail, a tuna-like fish. To develop the fish, researchers put a live fish under anesthesia and collected a sample of its muscle stem cells, the cells from which all other cells are grown. The fish was unharmed, but the researchers could then grow billions of cells from that sample by placing it in broths of nutrients, where the cells grew into muscle tissue. This "alternative seafood" is real fish flesh, just grown outside of a fish's body. BlueNalu CEO Lou Cooperhouse says, "The only difference from a BlueNalu fillet and a regular fish fillet is that we don't have the bones. We also don't have the mercury, the parasites, the micro-plastics, nor the bacteria these things are usually covered in." The fish is clean meat, tastes like the real thing, and harms no animals. A great deal more research will be necessary before such alternative fish comes to market, but BlueNalu hopes to begin selling it in the near future.

Quoted in Brittany Meiling, "Would You Eat Lab-Created Fish? This Startup Is Carving New Path in 'Alt-Meat' Industry," Phys.org, May 22, 2019. https://phys.org.

improve the meat and produce it in large quantities instead of in small petri dishes in the lab, this meat could mean the end of mass slaughter of animals while feeding the world.

This is just what companies like Memphis Meats are trying to do. In 2016 Memphis Meats produced the world's first meatball made from stem cells. In 2017 it made a chicken strip. And by 2018 the company was able to report that the cost of producing a quarter pound (113 g) of hamburger had been reduced from the initial $300,000 it cost to produce the first lab-grown burger in 2013 to $600. Taste has improved, too, with the addition of fat cells and careful selection of other meat cells. The company says it is impossible to tell that the meat is not real meat because it *is* real meat—just grown in a different way. Memphis Meats still needs to reduce the cost of its lab-grown meat and to produce it on a large scale, but it hopes to have a commercially viable product to introduce to the public within a few years.

If lab-grown meat becomes a reality, it could have a massive effect on the environment and on the way people eat. Marcus Johannes Post, the chief scientific officer of another lab-grown meat company called Mosa Meat, thinks that is a mission worth achieving. He explains:

If we can replace the majority of livestock meat production with cultured meat production, there would likely be enormous environmental benefits. One of the most devastating impacts of livestock production is that it entails mass deforestation. For example, around 70 percent of the Amazon rainforest has already been cleared for graz-

ing. . . . It is projected that cultured meat production will use 99 percent less land. . . . I am very excited about the prospect of cultured meat to do good for people and our planet.[25]

Tomorrow's Choices

In the future, people may have many alternatives to the meat of today. Whether they choose plant-based meat substitutes, insect meats, lab-grown meats, or other protein replacements, it is likely that their diets can be both environmentally friendly and more ethical and humane.

CHAPTER THREE

Genetic Engineering of Foods

In 2017 the first apples genetically altered to resist browning went on limited sale in the United States. Known as Arctic Goldens, these apples were developed from Golden Delicious apples by the company Okanagan Specialty Fruits. By 2019 the company was producing and marketing Arctic Fuji apples and Arctic Granny apples as well, all with the same nonbrowning trait. The apples are nutritious and tasty, but they do not brown when the flesh is exposed to air and do not bruise like ordinary apple varieties. They also help reduce food waste. In the United States almost half of all produce eventually ends up being thrown away, usually because it has gone bad. Arctic apples could ease this tremendous waste of food. Still, public reaction to the idea of the genetically altered food has been mixed. Stories about genetically altered foods often provoke strong reactions, partly because people are unclear about what genetically engineered foods actually are.

Genetically Modified

Most objections to genetically engineered foods arise because of the genetically modified organisms (GMOs) developed in the past. GMO technology became available in the United States in the 1990s and was the first form of genetic engineering. Scientists typically used other organisms, usually bacteria or viruses, to carry new genes into the nuclei of plant cells. There the new genes merged with the plant's genes so that new characteristics arose. Other approaches consisted of simply shooting extra genetic information directly into the cell's nucleus.

These techniques worked to change the DNA of the original plant. Scientists gave plants the ability to resist diseases caused by crop pests or to resist herbicides used to kill weeds where the plants were growing. These modified, pest-resistant, herbicide-resistant plants are superior crops for farmers to sow. They grow in difficult conditions, and crop yields are significantly better than for non-GMO crops.

In the United States today 94 percent of soybeans are GMOs, and government studies consistently report that they are safe to consume. Nevertheless, according to a 2018 Pew Research Center poll, about 50 percent of people say they do not want to eat GMO foods. At the same time, about thirty countries in the developed world either ban or restrict production of GMO foods.

Almost half of all produce in the United States ends up being thrown away because it has spoiled. Scientists are attempting to use genetic engineering to grow foods that resist spoiling.

Most of the rejection of GMOs is based on perceived threats to health, which the US government and most scientists dismiss. However, some scientists do worry about the small possibility of genes in foods transferring to human cells or the good bacteria in their digestive systems when people eat the GMO foods. Many GMO foods carry added genes that code for antibiotic resistance so that scientists can identify the altered plant cells easily. Those cells that carry resistance to antibiotics along with resistance to plant disease could perhaps pass on that antibiotic resistance to people. Those people would then be less responsive to antibiotics. No one has proved that such genetic transfer is possible, but the concern remains.

Other scientists and environmentalists worry about threats to the ecosystem. GMO technology is imprecise in that scientists have no control over where in the DNA of a plant the new genes are inserted. In addition, the added genes come from a different organism; they are not natural to the plant and therefore would never occur in natural plant reproduction. This could lead to unexpected modifications and traits that are not natural to the environment. Some are concerned that as GMO plants cross-pollinate with non-GMO plants, the crossbreeding will alter the DNA of the natural plants. No one knows what effect this might have on the ecosystem.

A Different Genetic Engineering

Although these concerns about GMO foods may someday be shown to be justifiable, the genetic engineering of today, such as that used to create Arctic apples, is quite different from past GMO technology. It is precise, uses no foreign genes from different organisms, and thus poses none of the risks to the environment or to people that older GMOs could. All that scientists do is alter a specific gene or piece of DNA in the plant's genome, much as could happen naturally in normal reproduction. The scientists can develop plants that grow better, require less acreage to produce larger crops, resist disease, taste better, or are more nutritious.

Arctic apples are a good example of how today's gene modification can be done. To understand the technique, it is necessary to understand why bruised or cut apples brown in the first place. On its website, Okanagan Specialty Fruits explains in a blog post:

> When the cell of a typical apple is ruptured—for example, by biting, slicing or bruising—polyphenol oxidase (PPO) found in one part of the cell mixes with polyphenolics found in another part of the cell. (PPO is a plant enzyme. Polyphenolics are one of the many types of chemical substrates that serve various purposes, including supplying its aroma and flavor.) When PPO and polyphenolics mix, brown-toned melanin is left behind.[26]

Scientists developed apples that do not brown by targeting the four genes that code for PPOs. Using a small piece of apple tissue in a petri dish in the lab, the scientists inserted a gene sequence

Gene Editing in Animals

Even farm animals may be gene edited in the future, both to improve their health and to reduce waste. Gene editing with animals and their complex genomes is much more difficult than it is with plants. As of 2019 the only gene-edited animal approved for human consumption is an Atlantic salmon. It has had two genes added to it from another fish species that make it grow bigger and faster. It has been on the market in Canada since 2017 and was approved by the FDA in 2019 for US sales. Other research in animals includes developing a tilapia fish that is gene edited to grow faster on fish farms; chickens that are resistant to avian flu, a contagious disease that can wipe out an entire flock; and pigs resistant to a serious disease called porcine reproductive and respiratory syndrome virus.

derived from apples in which the PPO genes have been turned off, or silenced. The silenced genes were placed exactly in the gene sequence where PPO genes belong and included gene markers that signal the new DNA sequence to start and stop appropriately. Okanagan Specialty Fruits says, "It's a precise, targeted gene modification that silences the PPO enzyme but doesn't change any other aspect of the cultivar [plant variety]." Then the lab tissue can be grown into a tiny plantlet. The company explains further:

> The Arctic apple plantlets are grown in the lab until they can be micrografted to apple rootstock to prepare them for planting. Total time from transformation to a young tree with fruit is approximately 24 months. . . . Once planted, Arctic apple trees grow at the same rate as conventional apples and don't require increased pesticide spraying or other special treatment in the orchard.[27]

Regular apples like this one turn brown and begin to rot when bruised. Genetically modified apples resist rotting even when they are bruised.

Gene Editing

Another method of precisely altering genes, called CRISPR/Cas9, has been used to make mushrooms that do not brown. This technology, known as gene editing, closely mimics natural genetic mutation. The CRISPR/Cas9 system uses an enzyme (a protein having a specific function) as a kind of molecular scissors that can precisely cut a DNA sequence in a particular gene. The cut is patched back together or repaired naturally by the cell. In 2015 Pennsylvania State University professor of plant pathology Yinong Yang used the CRISPR/Cas9 system to cut and delete a small sequence of one of the six genes that code for the production of PPOs in white button mushrooms. In effect, he created a gene mutation, and that alteration reduced the tendency of the mushroom to brown by 30 percent. In 2016 the US Department of Agriculture ruled that Yang's gene-edited button mushrooms did not have to be regulated as a GMO because there was nothing unnatural about them. Yang explains, "Our genome-edited mushroom has small deletions in a specific gene but contains no foreign DNA integration in its genome. . . . I hope development of the new technology will facilitate rational and productive dialogue among diverse groups of people, with a common goal to achieve food safety, food security, and agricultural and environmental sustainability."[28]

> "Our genome-edited mushroom has small deletions in a specific gene but contains no foreign DNA integration in its genome."[28]
>
> —Yinong Yang, a professor of plant pathology at Pennsylvania State University

As of 2020 the nonbrowning button mushrooms were not yet available for commercial sale. Yang and his team are seeking FDA approval. Even though such approval is not required for gene-edited foods, Yang believes that it will help consumers see the mushrooms as perfectly safe. Other gene-edited plants currently being researched include more nutritious tomatoes and corn, rice with increased yields, orange trees that are resistant to citrus greening disease, and wheat without gluten. Like Yang, many researchers believe that gene-editing technology is revolutionary. Luisa Bortesi, an agro-industrial biotechnology professor at Maastricht University in the Netherlands, asserts, "The question is not whether the use of programmable molecular scissors and other methods of genome editing to modify plants will have an impact on society, but when and where."[29]

Selective Breeding or Gene Editing?

A major reason scientists say that gene editing in agriculture should be widely accepted is that the technology is no different from the process of selective breeding that has been practiced for thousands of years—it is simply faster. Long before people understood genes or even knew what DNA is, they noticed the natural variations that occurred in the food plants and animals that they farmed. Natural variations in individual plants, for instance, occur frequently, caused by random mutations in the genes of the seed from which the plant grew. If that variation seemed desirable to a farmer, he or she would save the seeds from that plant to grow again. This is how, for example, the heavily seeded, hard, bitter wild variety of watermelon became the sweet, fleshy, sparsely seeded watermelon of today. Over a period of many years, humans selected the watermelon plant that had the fewest seeds in its fruit or a sweeter taste and grew only the seeds from that plant and its descendants. Both domestic plants and animals have been selectively bred for mutations that are useful in meeting people's needs. The foods people eat today are vastly genetically altered from the original species. Geneticist Alison Van Eenennaam explains, "We eat mutations every day. All the vegetables, grains, fruits and meat humans consume as part of

> "The question is not whether the use of programmable molecular scissors . . . will have an impact on society, but when and where."[29]
>
> —Luisa Bortesi, an agro-industrial biotechnology professor at Maastricht University

their diet are jam-packed with DNA speckled with mutations and beneficial variations."[30]

The difference that gene editing makes, whether with CRISPR/Cas9 technology or other methods, is that people now can breed food plants and animals precisely for the mutations they want. They do not have to wait for a useful variation to appear by accident. As Australian scientist and journalist Anna Salleh says, 'Gene editing means scientists can much more precisely target

Radioactivity and Food

People who object to genetic engineering of food crops are often unaware that many of the foods they think are natural are not natural at all. They were created through deliberate mutation breeding. Mutation breeding, also known as mutagenesis, is bombarding plants with radioactivity or chemicals to cause mutations in the genes. Some of these mutations turn out to be beneficial and desirable. The Ruby Red grapefruit, for instance, was developed with atomic radiation. The two most popular varieties, Star Ruby and Rio Red, are mutants developed in 1971 and 1985. A popular Japanese pear was experimented on for about twenty years with radiation until a mutant finally appeared in 1991 that was resistant to a black spot plant disease that was wiping out the crop. Today that pear variety is the most popular available in Japan. Many common wheat varieties, such as the kind used to make Italian pasta, were produced by being bombarded with radiation. In actuality, more than three thousand foods that are commonly eaten today were developed by blasting seeds with radiation to modify their genes. This includes many fruits, vegetables such as peas and lettuce, peanuts, and grains. Radiation causes mutations in many genes, while genetic engineering most often involves a deliberate, targeted mutation in only one. Yet mutagenesis is completely unregulated and typically unmentioned by people worried about consuming natural foods.

cut, delete and edit parts of the genome they want to change. So, no more wasting time creating a bunch of useless mutants!"[31]

Gene-Edited Bananas

With gene editing, undesirable variations are a nonissue, and reproduction of desirable mutations is completely predictable. Gene editing even holds the potential for increasing the nutritional value of foods that are selectively bred for taste. Bananas, for example, have been bred for their sweet taste, and modern bananas do not even produce seeds. More than 50 percent of the world's bananas are Cavendish bananas—yellow, easily peeled, sweet, and seedless. These bananas are nutritious, but they lack one very important nutrient: provitamin A. Provitamin A is turned into vitamin A in the body when foods rich in it are eaten. Vitamin A deficiency is common in many parts of the world and causes blindness and death in about half a million children each year. Yet in developing countries, such as many in Africa and Asia, bananas are a staple food source. Scientists wondered whether bananas could be genetically edited to solve this problem.

> "Gene editing means scientists can much more precisely target, cut, delete and edit parts of the genome they want to change."[31]
>
> —Anna Salleh, a scientist and journalist

The answer, as it turned out, was yes. At Queensland University of Technology in Australia, Professor James Dale announced in 2017 that he and his research team had succeeded in the quest for a supernutritious banana. Dale said, "What we've done is take a gene from a banana that originated in Papua New Guinea and is naturally very high in provitamin A but has small bunches and inserted it into a Cavendish banana."[32] This gene is still a natural banana gene; it is just from a wild variety that happens to retain the provitamin A gene. Dale's team is also researching adding the gene to Ugandan bananas, which are green cooking bananas

Bananas are a staple food in much of Africa and Asia. Scientists are working to make this food more nutritious.

that are a staple food in that country. Many Ugandans need more nutritious diets. Once commercially available, this gene-edited banana could save the sight and the lives of thousands, and the researchers hoped to be able to release the nutritious bananas to farmers in Uganda by 2021.

Improving the World's Staple Foods

Around the world, plant scientists are counting on gene editing to improve crops and feed the people of the future. In China, for instance, these scientists are conducting lab research with CRISPR/Cas9 for many staple food crops. Rice researcher Li Jiayang says, "We have to feed 1.4 billion people with very limited natural resources. We want to get the highest yield of production with the least input on the land from fertilizers and pesticides, and breed supervarieties that are pest and disease resistant as well as drought and salt tolerant. All this means we need to find the key genes and to work with them."[33] The challenge is that it is not easy to identify the multiple genes that may make a rice plant resistant to a certain disease or able to grow in drought conditions. Nevertheless, in 2019, researchers in the Philippines were able to identify and snip out three genes in a variety of rice that made it susceptible to a bacterial blight that can decimate rice crops in Africa and Asia. The research team was able to demonstrate in the laboratory that their gene-edited rice strongly resists the disease.

Chinese scientist Gao Caixia has developed a strain of wheat that grows particularly fat seeds and resists a common fungus infection called powdery mildew. Other scientists are working on corn plants that resist insect damage from corn earworms, while a biotechnology company called Calyxt has produced and is selling commercially a soybean oil for cooking that has been made healthier. Soybean oil is relatively healthy, but it is composed of saturated fats, as well as healthier polyunsaturated and monounsaturated fats. It even has a small amount of unhealthy trans fats. The new oil, named Calyno, has fewer saturated fats for heart health and zero trans fats. This gene-edited oil is now as healthy as olive oil but does not have olive oil's strong flavor. The company is also researching the development of wheat with less gluten for those who are sensitive to it, soy plants that are resistant to herbicides, and healthier potatoes that can be stored for longer periods. All of these food products are non-GMO. Instead, they are gene edited, selectively bred quickly and precisely through technology.

A Bright Future

While not everyone is enthusiastic about gene-editing technology, most researchers and geneticists are. They believe these techniques could solve any future problems with agricultural production and feeding the world. Science writer Clive Cookson argues that the technology "promises to transform agricultural production, for example genetically editing crops to make them resistant to disease or developing faster-growing varieties of livestock."[34] How quickly that transformation comes depends on the public's acceptance of gene editing and governments' willingness to approve the foods that result from it. Many believe, however, that genetic engineering will be a necessary part of the global agriculture of tomorrow.

CHAPTER FOUR

Personalized Diets

Today's dietary and nutritional guidelines, such as the US Department of Agriculture's ChooseMyPlate, are based on the average needs of the population as a whole. Yet each individual has slightly different needs that cannot be fully addressed by a one-size-fits-all dietary plan. Tim Spector, a professor of genetic epidemiology at King's College London in the United Kingdom, says, "In the world of nutrition, there's a real shift happening. People are finally starting to reject the notion that if everyone just follows the general guidelines (five servings of vegetables, counting calories, reducing fat) they'll be healthy forever."[35]

Determining Individual Needs

Spector and many researchers believe that the future of food and diet will include personal nutritional advice for each person. Scientists have discovered that each individual's nutritional needs are affected by several factors. A major factor is the genome—each person's complete DNA, including all the genes. Every individual has a unique genome, which may affect nutritional requirements.

Another factor is each person's unique microbiome. Every human body has a huge number of microorganisms living inside and outside. The microorganisms that live inside the body and the intestinal tract—sometimes called gut microbes—include bacteria, viruses, fungi, and other single-celled organisms. They are critical to metabolism (how the body digests and processes food), utilizing the nutrients in foods, and resisting disease. All of these microorganisms have their own genes, and these genes as a whole make up the microbiome. The microbiome, as well as the human genome, partially determines nutritional requirements. Finally, lifestyle plays a major role in nutritional needs. Factors such as level of exercise, one's daily schedule, and personal habits are important determinants of nutritional and dietary needs. All these variables together explain why each individual is different and has different food needs, both to maintain optimal health and to prevent, treat, or manage disease.

> "People are finally starting to reject the notion that if everyone just follows the general [dietary] guidelines . . . they'll be healthy forever."[35]
>
> —Tim Spector, a professor of genetic epidemiology at King's College London

Amazing Complexity in Personal Nutrition

The science of personal nutrition is still in its early stages, but scientists envision a day when the meals people eat will be based on knowledge of their specific metabolic, genetic, and lifestyle needs. Understanding these individual needs, however, is incredibly complex. In 2019 Spector and his team published the first results of the world's largest ongoing scientific nutrition study. The study, known as PREDICT, includes fourteen thousand sets of identical and nonidentical twins and measured factors such as blood sugar levels after a meal, insulin production by the pancreas in response to sugars and carbohydrates consumed, and fat levels in the blood. It looks at individual food preferences, activity levels, the times of day specific meals are eaten, and the quantity of food consumed at each meal. The first results are amazing even to the researchers. Spector reports, "The sheer scale and detail of our scientific project is such that for the first time we can explore tremendously rich nutrition data at the level of an individual. Our results surprisingly show that we are all different in our response to such a basic input as food. It was a real shock to see that even identical twins have such different responses."[36]

For all the study's participants, the researchers are finding large differences in the body's response to food depending on the time of day it was eaten. They find that individual increases of sugar and insulin in the blood are extremely variable from person to person, even when the same food is eaten at the same time.

Lifestyle factors such as exercise levels are important determinants of nutritional and dietary needs.

Some people show high levels of fats in the blood for hours after a meal, while others do not. Even the calories from foods are metabolized differently by different people.

Genetics do not account for these differences. Identical twins have almost the same genomes, but just as in the nonidentical population, their bodies' responses to food are very different, demonstrating that only about 33 percent of the differences are controlled by genes. Spector concludes, "We know that everybody is different in terms of their genetics, the chemicals they have in their body, and the species of microbes they have in their guts. These three factors vary widely between people and affect their response to food."[37]

How and Why Differences Matter

How and why individuals respond to food is important, not only for health and energy but also because issues like blood sugar levels affect whether someone may develop diabetes. Retaining fats in the blood may lead to heart disease, and responses to calories may determine weight gain or obesity. Yet little is known about how the microbiome affects such responses. Chemical differences in the body due to environmental factors, such as quantity of sleep or exercise, are equally important. Future PREDICT studies aim to explain the effects of all three factors that determine responses to food and to predict how each individual will respond to a specific food, meal, or diet plan. Spector says, "We believe that this ability to predict responses is the future of personalized nutrition."[38]

Spector also believes that the genetic tendency toward certain diseases or weight issues can be changed. Since most of the individual's responses to food are not genetic, people can learn to eat in the way that is healthiest for them. For example, some people metabolize their food most efficiently in the evening, rather than in the morning or throughout the day. Those people could decide to eat most of their food in the evening. Others might do best by eating five or six small meals throughout the day. Some people might need never to skip a meal; others might find that skipping meals helps them lose weight. Some people might be healthiest eating a low-fat diet; others might need a low-carbohydrate diet instead.

Personalized meal plans could improve health, and the effects of the microbiome on digestive health are changeable, too. That means that making the body's response to food better and healthier is possible. Spector explains, "We all have a unique set of gut microbes, but our gut microbiome is modifiable. This means that everybody can improve that gut health by picking the right foods or altering their environment, such as having more outdoor activities or getting a dog. You can change your microbiome within a few days with a dramatic change; it doesn't take years."[39] Exposure to pets leads to exposure to some of their bacteria, which seems to make the human microbiota more diverse and stronger. Spending time outdoors exposes people to more bacteria as well. Diverse microbiomes seem to be healthier for people and their food responses, but the science of the microbiome is still very new, and much more research

is needed before scientists will be able to advise people exactly how to behave and eat to have the best impact on health.

Nevertheless, the scientists working in the PREDICT project believe it will soon be possible to determine individual responses to food. One of the lead researchers, George Hadjigeorgiou, says, "We believe that everyone deserves to understand how they respond to food so that they can make confident decisions about what to eat and be in control of living a healthier and more enjoyable life."[40]

Providing Personalized Nutrition Advice

Although the PREDICT researchers do not believe they are ready to give individual nutritional advice, some private companies today are already offering personalized diet plans based on an individual's genome. By necessity, since it is based mostly on genes, the advice is somewhat generalized, but it is a first move toward personalized diets. Scientists have mapped the complete human genome and already can produce a genetic profile for each individual. In addition, some genetic information about individual dietary requirements has been identified.

In 2017 *Washington Post* journalist Sophie Egan decided to try one private company, Habit, that promised a personalized report on her dietary needs. First she performed a home test, including a cheek swab for a sample of her DNA and a high-fat, high-sugar, high-calorie beverage that she had to drink and then follow with

Eat Your Broccoli?

Genes help determine how bodies respond to food, and at the same time, foods can determine how some genes behave. Many genes in the body are either switched on or turned off in a process called gene regulation. Foods have the potential to affect gene regulation. Broccoli, for example, has chemical compounds that can switch on a particular gene that helps the body detoxify some toxic chemicals. So eating lots of broccoli not only provides an individual with healthful nutrients but also might protect that person if he or she is exposed to certain harmful chemicals in the environment. This beneficial effect, however, does not occur for all people. The gene that controls detoxifying chemicals is missing from about 20 percent of the population. It cannot be turned on by broccoli's chemical compounds, because it is not there. For these people, eating broccoli makes no difference. They still benefit from the nutrients in broccoli, of course, but the vegetable's detoxifying properties are of no benefit to them.

blood samples. She then mailed her results off to the company. When she received her report, Egan discovered that she was labeled as a person who could safely eat a wide variety of food choices; she was provided a daily calorie intake recommendation and a daily personal eating plan. The results did not include any particular disease risk for her, which was a great relief, but they did pinpoint a couple of genetic variations that suggested a need for a change in some food choices. Egan was uncertain how seriously to take those suggestions. She says:

> I'd be lying if I said the results haven't been affecting my food choices, or at least the way I feel about my food choices. For instance, since being told I have a genetic risk variant associated with slow production of omega-3s, I have been seeking salmon [a food high in omega-3] like a grizzly bear. Apparently, I'm also genetically predisposed to caffeine sensitivity. Many a morning, this news has me sitting at my desk thinking I must be tripping out on my cup of joe—despite the fact that I have consumed the exact same amount of coffee every day of my adult life.[41]

Egan was unsure whether she should stick to the personalized diet plan as a whole. She did not feel that the caffeine in her coffee bothered her and kept consuming the same amount. She could not decide whether to join friends and family in the meals they were eating or to stick with her recommended food choices only. She wonders, therefore, whether most people truly need and can feel comfortable with personalized diets.

Nutrigenomics Research

No one can yet answer Egan's concerns, but the emerging science known as nutrigenomics is trying to address those nutritional issues with precision. Nutrigenomics is the study of how food affects each individual's genes and how the genes determine the way each person reacts to different foods. Several DNA sequences have been identified as varying in different individuals, such as the caffeine sensitivity that Habit identified for Egan. Other known variations include how people process the cholesterol in foods they eat, how they metabolize starches, whether their bodies can digest lactose (a sugar molecule in milk), and how well their cells use some essential nutrients, such as folate (a B vitamin) and choline. About twenty different genes have been identified that influence whether people become obese. All of these genetic differences matter because in vulnerable individuals, they can lead to conditions such as heart disease, high blood pressure, or even vitamin deficiencies. Most genetic determinants of individual responses to foods ingested, however, remain unknown. So personalized diet plans of today, according to nutrition experts Mitch Kanter and Ashley Desrosiers, remain "illuminating but incomplete."[42]

Knowledge about the microbiome is even more incomplete. The genetic profile of the microbes inhabiting each person's body can be as much as 90 percent different between individuals. In addition, an individual's diet, health, and lifestyle

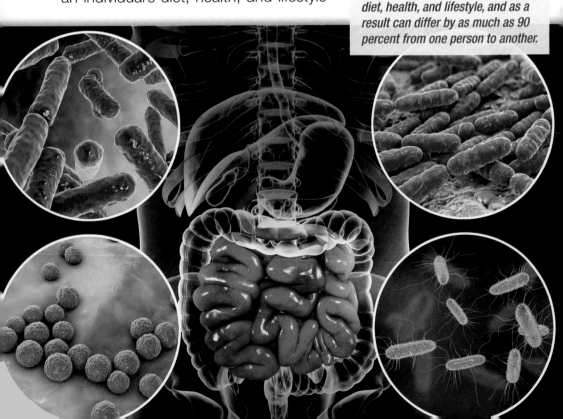

The microorganisms that inhabit the human body are affected by diet, health, and lifestyle, and as a result can differ by as much as 90 percent from one person to another.

affect the population of the microbiome more than its genetics. For example, people who eat a wide variety of fruits and vegetables have healthier digestive microbes than do people whose diet is more limited. And obese individuals have different microbial populations than do people of normal weight. Researchers know that the microbial population can change within an individual over time. They know that the microbes produce some vitamins critical to human health, as well as chemical compounds that help human bodies synthesize and absorb several other vitamins and miner-

Improving the Microbiome

In 2019 New Zealand scientist Aaron J. Stevens and his research team reported on their study on trying to change children's microbiomes. The small study included eighteen boys ages seven to twelve who were diagnosed with attention-deficit/hyperactivity disorder (ADHD). The researchers hypothesized that nutritional supplements could change the microbiome, making it healthier and thus also improving the behavioral and psychological problems in the children. The children were given capsules to swallow. Half of them received capsules with micronutrients chosen to feed the microbiome, and half received empty capsules so that their responses could be compared.

After ten weeks the researchers analyzed fecal samples from each of the children. Those receiving the micronutrient capsules had a more diverse microbiome than those who did not. The specific bacteria that other scientific studies have shown to be associated with ADHD were decreased. Although the study was small and more research is needed, the researchers are encouraged by their results. In a previous study, Stevens and the team determined that micronutrient treatments with one hundred ADHD children improved their attention and emotional responses. Now the team may know why. Micronutrients can change the microbiome, and changing the gut microbes may be one way to treat this common disorder in children.

als. However, researchers cannot yet determine how to change the microbe population with precision or determine exactly which microbes control health or the development of certain diseases or deficiencies. They cannot combine their knowledge of an individual's genome plus his or her microbiome to confidently develop personalized nutritional advice. That ability, say Kanter and Desrosiers, "is likely years away, but the future looks promising."[43]

Prescriptions for What to Eat

In the future, many nutrigenomics scientists predict that each person will be prescribed a specific personalized diet with precise nutritional recommendations for achieving and maintaining optimal health. Jeffrey Blumberg, a professor of nutrition science and policy at Tufts University in Massachusetts, predicts, "I'll be able to tell you what kinds of fruits, what kinds of vegetables and what kinds of whole grains that you should be choosing, or exactly how often. Or how about if I give you your own personalized K-Cup, so when you make your coffee in the morning, you're getting it with the key ingredients you need?"[44] Those key ingredients might include certain vitamin and mineral supplements. Much more research is needed. However, Blumberg says that some studies suggest that supplements could prevent some diseases, such as cancer or heart disease. People with genetic risk factors linked to those illnesses and a genetically increased need for certain vitamins could possibly protect their health with the supplements.

Jennie Brand-Miller, a professor of nutrition at the University of Sydney in Australia, concedes that current knowledge of personalized nutrition leaves much to be desired, but she is a proponent of the personalized nutrition plans offered today. She explains, "It's at an early stage [but] I think there's enough there at the moment for them to say, 'It's worth personalizing diets.' . . . I'm someone who wants to see people make positive changes to their lifestyle in order to improve quality of life and to reduce the health-care budget."[45] Already, scientists can identify gene variations and differences in metabolism linked to the microbiome and other factors that may increase risk for certain problems. The differences identified may not be precise or explain all the variables associated with response to food, but personalized dietary advice offers the opportunity to take charge of one's nutrition as no other diet recommendations do. Brand-Miller offers the example of perhaps preventing diabetes. She says, "Let's say a personalized diet company has shown that you've got a predisposition to diabetes; you've got 300 of the 400 gene mutations associated with getting Type-2 diabetes—it would then

Scientists are looking for ways to tailor balanced diets for the needs of individuals in order to achieve and maintain optimal health.

be important for you to take note of the most beneficial carbohydrate foods."[46] This kind of advice, she insists, is well worth acquiring.

A Rapidly Growing Science

Jose Ordovas, director of Nutrition and Genomics at Tufts University, knows that there are many more risks and needs to identify than diabetes or heart disease or even obesity, but he believes that precise individual dietary advice is coming. He explains, "Advances in science will increase the odds that a particular dietary pattern is successful for a particular individual. . . . The state of the science is growing all the time, and the degree to which diets can be personalized will continue to improve."[47] When that day comes, everyone will reap the benefits of a personalized diet that optimizes health.

"The state of the science is growing all the time, and the degree to which diets can be personalized will continue to improve."[47]

—Jose Ordovas, the director of Nutrition and Genomics at Tufts University

CHAPTER FIVE

New Ways to Eat

In the future, not only will people eat different kinds of foods and for different reasons, they will also have new ways to get food, prepare food, and even make foods tastier. No one can predict which foods will be fashionable years from now, but it is almost certain that change will come and that new inventions will revolutionize the ways food gets to the table and is enjoyed.

Reimagining Snack Food

One major driver behind the change in the way people eat in modern times is the population's demand for more convenient and healthier food options than traditional cook-from-scratch meals or fast-food options. In the food and restaurant industries, researchers are working to meet this demand. This does not mean simply protein bars or cookies with no trans fats but a real transformation in food choices. In Singapore, for instance, a company called NamZ is redesigning instant noodles. Such noodles are an extremely popular comfort food in Asia, and in the Western world, they are common snacks. They are not, however, particularly healthy. They are usually deep-fried in palm oil and made with nutritionally inadequate white flour. The cofounder of NamZ, Christoph Langwallner, says, "Our current food system is feeding us into obesity, type-2 diabetes, cardiovascular diseases and more with calorie-dense but nutrient-poor food. . . . We are looking for opportunities to redesign comfort food in order to create a significant health impact."[48]

The company's first offering is named NoodleZ. These instant noodles have 70 percent less fat than regular noodles and are made with healthy oils. Instead of white flour, the noodles are made with nontraditional crops, including the highly nutritious leaves of a drought-resistant tree called moringa and a peanut-like plant called Bambarra groundnut. People who have tasted NoodleZ say they cannot tell the difference between them and regular instant noodles, but NoodleZ are a much healthier snack option. NamZ was planning to launch its new product in Singapore and Malaysia in 2020 and hopes to expand the market in the future. It is also working on developing a high-protein version, with 136 percent more protein and 83 percent more fiber than traditional instant noodles.

In the United States a Japanese company known as Base Food is partnering with Ramen Nagi, the successful instant noodle

> "We are looking for opportunities to redesign comfort food in order to create a significant health impact."[48]
>
> —Christoph Langwallner, the cofounder of NamZ

Instant noodles are a common, but not particularly healthy, type of fast food in Asia and the Western world.

producer, to introduce healthy noodles, too. Base Noodles are nutritionally superior to traditional ramen noodles. They have 29 grams of protein and 8 grams of fiber per serving and provide one-third of an adult's daily requirement of vitamins and minerals Chef Satoshi Ikuta of the Ramen Nagi restaurant in California says 'Our collaboration with Base Food reflects our mission to connect the world through noodles, by expanding the deliciousness and

Neurogastronomy

Neurogastronomy is an emerging science that studies how the brain processes information from taste, smell, hearing, sight, and touch to determine the flavors people perceive in food. It asks why some foods are perceived to be more delicious than others and whether that perception can be changed. Scientists believe that someday an understanding of how people perceive flavor could enable them to trick their brains into believing that carrots or broccoli are more delicious than candy. It could help people reduce sugar intake by tricking the brain into tasting more sweetness than is there. It could even help cancer patients who have lost their taste due to chemotherapy enjoy their meals again.

At his Fat Duck Restaurant in London, Chef Heston Blumenthal demonstrates to his clients how neurogastronomy works. The restaurant's seafood dish is served on a platter that looks like sand and seaweed and smells salty. MP3 players are at each table, playing sounds of the sea. All of the diners' senses are engaged, and their enjoyment of the meals is greatly enhanced. Their perception of saltiness is enhanced as well, even though Blumenthal uses less salt in his creation than is typical. In the future, predict neurogastronomists, perhaps people will use digital imagery headsets to make their food taste wonderful. They may eat barbecued ribs while in a Texas landscape or eat seafood at a virtual reality beach, all without ever leaving their kitchen tables.

fun that can only be achieved with ramen. We want to push the boundaries of ramen to spread its taste and enjoyment to as many people as possible; this collaboration is one exciting example of this."[49] Nutritious noodles may be one of the first steps toward a future in which good health does not have to be sacrificed in order to enjoy delicious convenience in snack foods.

No Waste and Perfectly Fresh

The grocery industry is also working toward convenience in food-buying choices, particularly in food packaging that helps prevent waste and ensures freshness. Scientists have developed intelligent packaging for fresh foods that can monitor the food and detect its quality and whether it is still good to eat. Such packaging is not yet in widespread use, but in the future it will likely be in every grocery store, allowing consumers to choose meats, bakery products, fruits, and vegetables at peak freshness. At home the packaging will signal the food's status to the consumer. Patricia Müller and Markus Schmid, life science professors at Albstadt-Sigmaringen University in Germany, explain why this development is important. They say:

> "In fear groceries could be spoiled, many consumers throw products away which would actually have still been suitable for consumption."[50]
>
> —Patricia Müller and Markus Schmid, life science professors at Albstadt-Sigmaringen University in Germany

Depending on the contents of the package, biological, chemical, or physical processes occur, which ultimately lead to spoilage of the product. These changes are in most cases difficult to assess by the consumers. In fear groceries could be spoiled, many consumers throw products away which would actually have still been suitable for consumption. Often a small deviation from the norm, either the color, the consistency, or even the passing of the best before date leads to products ending up in the [trash] bin.[50]

In the United States, for example, people throw away some 150,000 tons (136,078 metric tons) of food daily. Much food loss could be avoided and the world's food supply enhanced with intelligent packaging.

At Imperial College London in 2019, a research team developed sensors called paper-based electrical gas sensors (PEGS) that are printed on paper and can detect gases that are emitted by fish and meat as they are going bad. The sensors are combined with microchips that can be read by smartphones. If a consumer wanted to know whether the meat or fish in the refrigerator was safe to eat, he or she could simply hold the phone up to the packaging and get the answer. Head researcher Firat Güder explains, "Our vision is to use PEGS in food packaging to reduce unnecessary food waste and the resulting plastic pollution. . . . Citizens want to be confident that their food is safe to eat, and to avoid throwing food away unnecessarily because they aren't able to judge its safety. These sensors are cheap enough that we hope supermarkets could use them within three years."[51] The researchers also plan to apply the PEGS model to other types of food in the future, such as signaling gases emitted by spoiling vegetables.

Inventing Healthy, Convenient Sweets

Health and safety are likely to play remarkable roles in the ways people eat in the future. Researchers in Spain, for instance, are experimenting with turning chocolate into a medicine. The research is still confined to the laboratory, but scientists have long known that certain chemical compounds in chocolate, known as flavonoids, have health benefits for people. One of those benefits is the ability to lower blood pressure. The Spanish researchers altered cocoa powder to make it particularly rich in flavonoids. Then they tested this cocoa powder in rats. Rats get high blood pressure just as people do and respond to the same kinds of blood pressure drugs. The scientists fed the cocoa powder to rats, some with high blood pressure and some with normal blood pressure. They compared the results to those of a common blood

Researchers are working on developing chocolate that will taste good but will resist melting and creating a mess in the warmth of a person's pocket.

pressure medication. The cocoa powder worked just as well as medicine to lower the rats' blood pressure. At the same time, it had no bad effects on the rats with normal blood pressure. Of course, next the researchers have to study the chocolate's effects in people, but someday, people may simply eat a couple of squares of chocolate every day to control high blood pressure.

That chocolate may not even melt until it is in the consumer's mouth, if food industry researchers have their way. The chocolatier Barry Callebaut has invented a chocolate, known as Choc37.9, that does not melt in hands, pockets, or purses. The ingredients that make this feat possible are being kept secret, but the chocolate company is already selling its invention in some parts of the world. Busy people who want to eat a chocolate snack while commuting or walking to their next class would have no problems with sticky messes. In addition, this chocolate can be sold and eaten in tropical places. Bas Smit, the company's head of marketing, explains, "Our new Choc37.9 offers great potential for tasty chocolate experiences in warmer climates. Products can be displayed in stores, there is no need any more for cooled transportation in certain areas and the whole logistic process in general is simplified enormously."[52]

DouxMatok, an Israeli company, has developed a process to make sugar taste sweeter and salt taste saltier, which can reduce the amount of sugar and salt people consume. This process may help people in the future avoid health problems caused by the amount of sugar and salt in their foods. It involves coating mineral particles with sugar or salt. The company explains:

> We use a mineral carrier, load it with sugar or salt, creating clusters of sweetness or saltiness. These clusters are heavier, stay longer at the taste receptors [in the mouth], and more efficiently deliver salt or sugar to their respective taste receptors. The download of the sugars or salt is consequently made at the right place at the right time, resulting in a higher perception of sugar/salt.[53]

As of 2019 this technology was still in the research stage. Someday soon, however, the sweet snacks people buy—whether doughnuts or cookies or pie—may contain 40 percent less sugar than they do today while still tasting just as sweet. This could mean fewer calories and more guilt-free desserts in the future.

Robots in the Kitchen

The kinds of foods people buy will be different in the future, and so will the way food is prepared. According to most engineers, the future lies in robotics, and that does not just mean manufacturing robots, driverless cars, and self-propelling vacuum cleaners.

Robots are coming to the kitchen, too. Stuart Farrimond, medical doctor, food scientist, and author, predicts, "Imagine being able to send a message [to] your Robo-Chef while on the commute home to prepare a recipe of your choice. Within moments, android arms will be gathering ingredients from the fridge, julienning the turnips and deboning the chicken."[54]

In the United Kingdom the company Moley Robotics has already developed what it calls the world's first robotic kitchen. The company announces on its website, "This is the future and it is here today." Moley advertises, "Featuring an advanced, fully functional robot integrated into a beautifully designed, professional kitchen, it cooks with the skill and flair of a master chef. [And it] will be supported by an iTunes' style library of recipes."[55] The Robochef comes

Less Salt with Nanotechnology

Scientists today are researching ways to make food healthier with the use of nanoparticle technology. At Nottingham University in the United Kingdom, researchers have figured out a way to break down salt crystals into minute nanoscale particles. This increases the surface of each salt particle so that the flavor is perceived more easily and quickly by human taste buds. That means increasing the saltiness of foods without increasing the salt. The researchers coated potato chips with these nanoparticles and gave them to volunteers to try. Even though the chips had 90 percent less salt than a normal potato chip, the volunteers could not tell the difference. Since too much salt in the diet can adversely affect health, such technology may be used in the future to create healthy but satisfyingly salty snack foods.

with a 3-D camera to "see" and a pair of articulated, or jointed arms. For safety, it is enclosed within a glass-surrounded cooking station, complete with a stove, refrigerator, and sink. It is equipped with a set of prepackaged containers of ingredients already measured, washed, and cut. The robotic "hands" wear gloves covered with sensors that can combine ingredients, mix, stir, and use a food processor. The Robochef cooks the meal and can even clean up the dishes in the sink when meal preparation is done. Then its arms retract out of sight until the next time they are needed.

For now, the Robochef's menu capability is about one hundred recipes, but in the future, Moley expects to be able to expand the library of recipes almost without limit. The founder and CEO of Moley Robotics, Mark Oleynik, says, "Our dream is not only to introduce the fully automated Moley robotic kitchen into the marketplace, but to bring the cost down to a point where it is affordable for the middle class. I am personally entirely confident we will make this dream a reality."[56] The Moley Robotics kitchen is not yet available for sale, and its expected cost is about $15,000.

Perhaps its initial use will be in restaurants rather than homes, but someday everyone may be freed from cooking while enjoying chef-quality meals prepared at home.

Or Just Print Your Food

Another possibility for future home cooking involves 3-D printer technology. A food 3-D printer works like a regular 3-D printer for making plastic toys or similar products, but instead of plastic, it uses edible ingredients in a paste or powder form that are extruded from a nozzle onto a building plate. Chocolate, for instance, is one of the first foods to be used in 3-D printing. The chocolate paste is heated in the nozzle tube and then extruded layer by layer onto the plate. As it cools, it hardens into as intricate a pattern as one desires. For candymakers, the printer is a boon because no molds are necessary to make their fancy-looking chocolate candies. Some European candy shops are already using 3-D printers to produce intricate chocolate candies to sell to their customers.

Food printers of today, however, with their multiple nozzles, can do much more than make pretty candy. Almost any food that can be pureed or turned into a paste can become the "ink" in a 3-D food printer. In London, for example, a restaurant called Food Ink bills itself as "the world's first 3D printing restaurant."[57] Everything in the restaurant is printed—tables, chairs, utensils, wall decorations, and nine courses of food. The restaurant is so popular that it is extremely difficult to get a reservation, but the printed food has one drawback: it cannot be cooked in the printer. Another 3-D printer company in Columbus, Ohio, called BeeHex has the same issue. Using multiple nozzles for sauce, cheese, and dough, it builds a pizza with 3-D printers, but once made, the pizza has to be put into an oven to be baked. Nevertheless, the company plans to sell its pizza printer in restaurants and homes as a convenient, fast alternative for a fresh pizza that is ready in only five minutes.

Foodini, a 3-D printer from the company Natural Machines, is already available at a cost of about $4,000 to anyone who wants to print food at home. Users can load their own ingredients to make dishes such as guacamole, pancakes, pizza, cookies, crackers, and ravioli. Although the company expects Foodini to be most appealing to restaurants at first, it predicts that within fifteen years, the appliance will be as common in homes as a microwave or conventional oven is today. To those who wonder why anyone would want to print their food, Natural Machines says:

> Today, too many people eat too much convenience foods, processed foods, packaged foods, or pre-made meals— many with ingredients that are unidentifiable to the common consumer, versus homemade, healthy foods and snacks. But there is the problem of people not having enough time to make homemade foods from scratch. Enter Foodini. Foodini is a kitchen appliance that takes on the difficult parts of making food that is hard or time-consuming to make fully by hand. By 3D printing food, you automate some of the assembly or finishing steps of home cooking, thus making it easier to create freshly made meals and snacks.[58]

Although Foodini cannot cook foods, the company is researching ways to make cooking possible in the future. A research team at Columbia University in New York has already invented a food printer in its lab that can cook. The printer is equipped with six nozzles and an infrared lamp. The team says, "Integrating an infrared lamp heating mechanism into the printer allows for more precise spatial control of the heat being delivered to printed food, the ability to create complex food patterns with more ingredient complexity, and the integration of multiple food ingredients in a single 3D object."[59]

"Foodini is a kitchen appliance that takes on the difficult parts of making food that is hard or time-consuming to make fully by hand."[58]

—Natural Machines, a 3-D food printer company

New Food Adventures Coming

No one knows for sure whether people in the future will eat food made only with healthy, natural ingredients, packaged to ensure freshness, and cooked specifically for them by their robochefs or artistically prepared with their own kitchen printers. Whatever innovations and developments are coming, however, scientists do predict that the way we eat will never be the same.

SOURCE NOTES

Introduction: Future Food Issues

1. Juergen Voegele and Jane Nelson, "4 Priorities in the Race to Build a Sustainable Global Food System," World Economic Forum Annual Meeting, January 18, 2019. www.weforum.org.
2. Institute on the Environment, "Is There Enough Food for the Future?," 2016. www.environmentreports.com.
3. Scottish Food Coalition, "Food and the Environment: How What We Eat Impacts the Planet," 2017. www.foodcoalition.scot.
4. Voegele and Nelson, "4 Priorities in the Race to Build a Sustainable Global Food System."

Chapter One: How the World Gets Its Food

5. Food and Agriculture Organization of the United Nations, "The Future of Food and Agriculture: Alternative Pathways to 2050," January 9, 2018. www.fao.org.
6. Union of Concerned Scientists, "What Is Sustainable Agriculture?," April 10, 2017. www.ucsusa.org.
7. Quoted in Jason Johnson, "#Fridaysonthefarm: Iowa Farmer Uses Roller Crimper in Organic No-Till System," Natural Resources Conservation Service, July 28, 2017. www.nrcs.usda.gov.
8. Quoted in Winsome Denyer, "Soaking Up Australia's Drought," ABC News, December 3, 2018. www.abc.net.au.
9. Quoted in Alex Rea, "Landscape Rehydration Project Rewarded with $3.8M Grant," About Regional, April 3, 2019. https://aboutregional.com.au.
10. Farm Health Online, "Antibiotics in Agriculture: Can We Reduce Antibiotic Usage?," 2018. www.farmhealthonline.com.

11. Allen Williams and Russ Conser, "What to Tell Environmentalists About Cows," *Graze*, April 1, 2018. www.grazeonline .com.

12. Quoted in Chicken Check In, "How Terry Baker Practices Environmental Sustainability on His Farm," 2015. www.chicken check.in.

13. Chicken Check In, "Sustainability: How Does Chicken Production Impact the Environment? How Is the Chicken Industry Minimizing Its Environmental Impact?," 2015. www.chicken check.in.

14. Quoted in North Carolina State University. "Aquaculture Does Little, If Anything, to Conserve Wild Fisheries," ScienceDaily, February 11, 2019. www.sciencedaily.com.

15. Quoted in Maddie Oatman, "A Fish Out of Water: Can Farmers in Iowa Help Save the World's Seafood Supply?," *Mother Jones*, January/February 2017. www.motherjones.com.

Chapter Two: Meat Alternatives

16. Quoted in Ashley Lutz, "Why McDonald's Doesn't Sell Veggie Burgers," Business Insider, January 5, 2015. www.business insider.com.

17. Quoted in Joseph Hincks, "Meet the Founder of Impossible Foods, Whose Meat-Free Burgers Could Transform the Way We Eat," *Time*, April 23, 2018. https://time.com.

18. Quoted in Stephan J. Bronner, "With $72 Million in Funding, the Entrepreneur Behind Beyond Meat Pursues Innovation over Profit," *Entrepreneur*, January 22, 2018. www.entrepre neur.com.

19. Quoted in Zachary Mack, "Beyond Meat CEO Ethan Brown on How Meatless Burgers Can Still Improve," The Verge, January 13, 2019. www.theverge.com.

20. Quoted in Amy Murphy, "Insects Are 'Food of the Future,'" *Ecologist*, July 2, 2019. https://theecologist.org.

21. Quoted in Jane Alice Liu, "Insect Farming: How Insects Help Reduce Food Waste," Food Unfolded, 2019. www.foodun folded.com.

22. Quoted in Ruqayyah Moynihan and Christoph Damm, "Two German Guys Figured Out How to Get People to Eat Insect Burgers," Business Insider, May 16, 2018. www.business insider.com.

23. Kendrick Foster, "Bread and Butter and . . . Bugs?," *Harvard Political Review*, March 8, 2019. https://harvardpolitics.com.

24. Quoted in Foster, "Bread and Butter and . . . Bugs?"

25. Quoted in Luke Dormehl, "Burgers Are Just the Beginning: Embracing the Future of Lab-Grown Everything," Digital Trends, April 22, 2019. www.digitaltrends.com.

Chapter Three: Genetic Engineering of Foods

26. Okanagan Specialty Fruits, "How'd We 'Make' a Nonbrowning Apple?," *Arctic Apples Blog*, 2020. www.arcticapples .com.

27. Okanagan Specialty Fruits, "PPO Silencing: How We Do It," 2020. www.okspecialtyfruits.com.

28. Quoted in Chuck Gill, "Penn State Developer of Gene-Edited Mushroom Wins 'Best of What's New' Award," Penn State News, October 19, 2016. https://news.psu.edu.

29. Luisa Bortesi, "Tailor-Made Plants Using Next-Generation Molecular Scissors," The Bridge, National Academy of Engineering, March 15, 2018. www.nae.edu.

30. Alison Van Eenennaam, "Gene-Edited Food Regulations: Whether It's a Plant or Animal Shouldn't Matter, but It Does Now," The Conversation, February 26, 2019. https://thecon versation.com.

31. Anna Salleh, "CRISPR Editing of Plants and Animals Gets Green Light in Australia. Now What?," ABC News, April 29, 2019. www.abc.net.au.

32. Quoted in Karl Gruber, "Genetically Modified Produce—Misunderstood Wonders," Phys.org, February 1, 2018. https:// phys.org.

33. Quoted in Jon Cohen, "To Feed Its 1.4 Billion, China Bets Big on Genome Editing of Crops," *Science*, July 29, 2019. www. sciencemag.org.

34. Clive Cookson, "Why the Future of Gene-Edited Foods Is in the Balance," *Financial Times*, March 11, 2019. www.ft.com.

Chapter Four: Personalized Diets

35. Quoted in Medical News Today, "Nutrition: Even Identical Twins Respond Differently to Food," June 20, 2019. www.medicalnewstoday.com.

36. Quoted in ZOE, "When It Comes to Food, One Size Doesn't Fit All: World's Largest Scientific Nutrition Research Project Reveals Even Identical Twins Have Different Responses to Food," EurekAlert! June 10, 2019. www.eurekalert.org.

37. Quoted in Molly Campbell and Karen Steward, "You're Unique, So Your Nutrition Should Be Too: An Interview with Professor Tim Spector," Technology Networks, November 1, 2019. www.technologynetworks.com.

38. Quoted in Campbell and Steward, "You're Unique, So Your Nutrition Should Be Too."

39. Quoted in Campbell and Steward, "You're Unique, So Your Nutrition Should Be Too."

40. Quoted in ZOE, "When It Comes to Food, One Size Doesn't Fit All."

41. Sophie Egan, "I Sent in My DNA to Get a Personalized Diet Plan. What I Discovered Disturbs Me," special to the *Washington Post*, *Chicago Tribune*, August 19, 2017. www.chicagotribune.com.

42. Mitch Kanter and Ashley Desrosiers, "Personalized Wellness Past and Future: Will the Science and Technology Coevolve?," *Nutrition Today*, July 17, 2019. https://journals.lww.com.

43. Kanter and Desrosiers, "Personalized Wellness Past and Future."

44. Quoted in Clare Leschin-Hoar, "Nutrition Gets Personal: Dietary Guidance That's Targeted to Your Precise Genetic Makeup Is the Wave of the Future, Says Nutrition Scientist Jeffrey Blumberg," Portside, July 20, 2015. www.portside.org.

45. Quoted in Chris Bourn, "Are Personalized Diets the Only Kind That Work?," MEL Magazine, July 31, 2019. https://melmagazine.com.

46. Quoted in Bourn, "Are Personalized Diets the Only Kind That Work?"

47. Quoted in Health & Nutrition Letter, "Personalized Nutrition," April 2019. www.nutritionletter.tufts.edu.

Chapter Five: New Ways to Eat

48. Quoted in Guan Yu Lim, "Sustainable Noodles: Singapore Start-Up Creating Comfort Food with 'Future Fit Crops,'" Food Navigator-Asia, December 16, 2019. www.foodnavigator-asia.com.

49. Quoted in Daniel Hutson, "Base Food Partners with Ramen Nagi to Showcase Nutritionally-Balanced Noodles with Flavorful Flair," Business Wire, August 29, 2019. www.businesswire.com.

50. Patricia Müller and Markus Schmid, "Intelligent Packaging in the Food Sector: A Brief Overview," Foods, MDPI, January 7, 2019. www.mdpi.com.

51. Quoted in Imperial College London, "Food Freshness Sensors Could Replace 'Use-By' Dates to Cut Food Waste," ScienceDaily, June 5, 2019. www.sciencedaily.com.

52. Quoted in QSR Media UK, "Barry Callebaut Introduces 'Melt in Your Mouth, Not Your Hand' Chocolate," February 23, 2016. https://qsrmedia.co.uk.

53. DouxMatok, "Technology Platform," 2017. www.douxmatok.com.

54. Stuart Farrimond, "The Future of Food: What We'll Eat in 2028," Science Focus, May 17, 2019. www.sciencefocus.com.

55. Moley Robotics, "Future Is Served." www.moley.com.

56. Quoted in PYMNTS, "Moley and Robo Chef Magic," October 31, 2018. www.pymnts.com.

57. Quoted in Chiara Cecchini, "Edible Carving: The World's First 3D Printing Restaurant," The Spoon, October 21, 2018. https://thespoon.tech.

58. Natural Machines, "FAQ," 2020. www.naturalmachines.com.
59. Quoted in Jack Colyer, "Columbia University 3D Printed Food Challenges Conventional Flavor Profiles," 3D Printing Industry, April 15, 2019. https://3dprintingindustry.com.

Books

Tennille Nicole Allen, *Food Inequalities*. Health and Medical Issues Today. Santa Barbara, CA: Greenwood, 2020.

DK, *The Story of Food: An Illustrated History of Everything We Eat*. London: DK, 2018.

Kaitlyn Duling, *Droughts and Crop Failure*. 21st-Century Engineering Solutions for Climate Change. New York: Cavendish Square, 2018.

MK Grassi, *Let's Eat Bugs! A Thought-Provoking Introduction to Edible Insects for Adventurous Teens and Adults*. 2nd ed. CreateSpace, 2014.

Space10, *Future Food Today: A Cookbook*. Amsterdam: Frame, 2019.

Whitney Stewart and Hans Andersson, *Genomics: A Revolution in Health and Disease Discovery*. Minneapolis: Twenty-First Century, 2020.

Molly Watson, *Should We All Be Vegan? A Primer for the 21st Century*. London: Thames & Hudson, 2019.

Internet Sources

American Museum of Natural History, "Future of Food." www.amnh.org.

Genetic Science Learning Center, "The Human Microbiome," August 15, 2014. https://learn.genetics.utah.edu.

Franklin Houser, "3D Printed Food: A Culinary Guide to 3D Printing Food," ALL3DP, August 29, 2017. https://all3dp .com.

Tanya Lewis, "Here's What Fruits and Vegetables Looked Like Before We Domesticated Them," Science Alert, September 20, 2018. www.sciencealert.com.

Amanda Mah, "CRISPR in Agriculture: An Era of Food Evolution," Synthego, March 28, 2019. www.synthego.com.

Websites

Bugible (https://bugible.com). Billing itself as "the leading bug blog in North America," this site introduces people to the idea of eating insects. It offers articles on many aspects of insect-eating, including the need to get kids excited about eating bugs.

Food and Agriculture Organization of the United Nations (www.fao.org). Major topics at the Food and Agriculture Organization website include climate change, sustainable food and agriculture, the future of food, and conservation.

FoodPrint (https://foodprint.org). A project of the Grace Communications Foundation, FoodPrint is dedicated to increasing public awareness of food and environmental issues. The website offers many articles about issues such as climate change, raising livestock and crops sustainably, and what the public can do to help protect the environment.

Moley Robotics (www.moley.com). Watch the Moley Robochef cook a meal and read about the technology involved at the Moley Robotics website.

Young People's Trust for the Environment (https://ypte.org .uk). This nonprofit British organization encourages young people to understand the need for sustainability in the environment. Click on the link for teens to learn about climate change, ocean pollution, and other issues. Browse the fact sheets under "F" to read about food of the future.

INDEX

PICTURE CREDITS

ABOUT THE AUTHOR

Toney Allman holds degrees from Ohio State University and the University of Hawaii. She currently lives in Virginia, where she enjoys a rural lifestyle as well as researching and writing about a variety of topics for students.